Fact Finders®

CRACKING
THE **MEDIA**
LITERACY
CODE

UNDERSTANDING ✶ ✶ ✶ ✶ PROPAGANDA ✶

BY JOHN MICKLOS JR.

CONSULTANT:
ROBERT L. MCCONNELL, PHD

CAPSTONE PRESS
a capstone imprint

Fact Finders Books are published by Capstone Press
1710 Roe Crest Drive, North Mankato, Minnesota 56003
www.mycapstone.com

Library of Congress Cataloging-in-Publication Data
Names: Micklos, John, author.
Title: Understanding propaganda / by John Micklos Jr.
Description: North Mankato, Minnesota : Capstone Press, [2019] |
  Series: Fact finders. Cracking the media literacy code. | Includes index.
Identifiers: LCCN 2018001960 (print) | LCCN 2018004809 (ebook)
  ISBN 9781543527216 (eBook PDF)
  ISBN 9781543527056 (hardcover)
  ISBN 9781543527131 (pbk.)
Subjects: LCSH: Propaganda--Juvenile literature.
Classification: LCC HM1231 (ebook) | LCC HM1231 .M53 2019 (print) | DDC 303.3/75--dc23
LC record available at https://lccn.loc.gov/2018001960

Editorial Credits
Michelle Bisson, editor; Russell Griesmer, designer; Jennifer Bergstrom, production artist; Morgan Walters,
media researcher; Tori Abraham, production specialist

Photo Credits
Alamy: The Advertising Archives, 15; Getty Images: ALI AL-SAADI, 19, Fine Art, left 23, Interim Archives,
13, NurPhoto, 27; Library of Congress: Prints and Photographs Division, top 14; Newscom: Berliner Verlag/
Archiv/picture alliance / ZB, 5, Everett Collection, 16, Iain Findlay/Mirrorpix, 6, Ken Welsh, 12, MIKE
BLAKE/REUTERS, 7, Mondadori Portfolio, bottom 14, Patsy Lynch/Polaris, 9, Robin Alam/Icon Sportswire
164, 28; Bottom of Form Shutterstock: Alisara Zilch, design element throughout, Anton Watman, 10, balabolka,
design element throughout, Eladora, (head) Cover, 1, George Sheldon, 21, Georgejmclittle, 25, Joseph Sohm,
22, right 23, Macrovector, design element throughout, topform, design element throughout

Printed in the United States of America.
PA021

TABLE OF CONTENTS

CHAPTER 1

PROPAGANDA: WHAT IS IT?

Adolf Hitler believed that blond, blue-eyed people were better than anyone else. He thought other people were not as good and should be killed. He and his Nazi party used slogans such as "master race" to make some Germans feel better than other people. The Nazis did this in the years before and during World War II (1939-1945). They claimed to be simply building a sense of national pride. But the terms were part of a broad propaganda campaign.

Propaganda is a form of communication used to affect other people's thoughts and actions. Hitler hated Jewish people. He and his Nazi followers spread lies about Jews. They unfairly blamed Jewish people for various problems in Germany. Student schoolbooks also portrayed Jewish people as evil.

The Germans used propaganda posters to further their cause.

Over time many Germans came to believe the lies. Most people didn't object when the Nazis passed laws keeping Jews from being German citizens or marrying Germans. Nor did they speak out when Jewish people were sent to concentration camps. Eventually the Nazis killed about 6 million Jews. It became known as the Holocaust. It's one of the most horrific examples of how effective propaganda can be and why we must understand it.

 Enlighten or Misinform?

The name of the Nazi ministry that spread misinformation was the Ministry of Public Enlightenment and Propaganda. *Enlighten* means to shine light on the truth. Instead the ministry used lies to mislead German citizens.

★ propaganda—information spread to try to influence the thinking of people; often not completely true or fair

Propaganda seeks to control what people believe. Political parties use it to back candidates or plans. People may use it to back or make fun of a certain religion. Even governments use it. In all cases, the goal is the same. Those who spread propaganda want to change people's beliefs. Once they've done that, they hope to change people's actions.

In today's world we are flooded with information every day. How can we tell when it is propaganda? It's propaganda when only certain facts are presented or when statements are twisted to suit a certain point of view. It's propaganda if the information is false.

Think about any issue that people argue about. Those who support gun control, for example, may use only those statistics that support their point of view. The same is true for those who oppose it. Issues such as the death penalty and immigration draw similar heated debate.

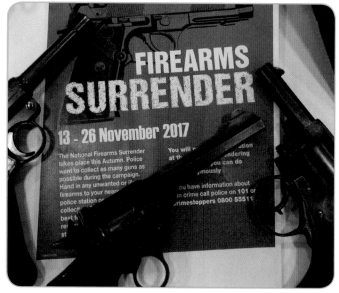

People in the U.S. feel very strongly—for and against—gun ownership.

People often use simple slogans on signs when they demonstrate about an issue.

Just because information is propaganda doesn't mean that the point it's trying to make is wrong. In fact, there are cases where propaganda is good, just as there are cases where it's bad.

All propaganda aims to influence people's opinions and change their actions. How, then, can we determine when it is good and when it's bad? One key is its purpose. Does it promote a good cause?

One example: Years ago cigarette companies used propaganda tools to encourage young people to smoke. They tried to make smoking look cool. It's an example of bad propaganda. They deceived the public by hiding information about health dangers linked to smoking.

Today public service campaigns try to raise awareness about the dangers of smoking. The campaigns encourage young people not to smoke. Some of the ads are quite graphic. They show young people losing their teeth or skin because of smoking. They depict older people breathing through tubes because of cancer caused by their smoking. Although based on fact, the ads are exaggerated to have the biggest effect. This is good propaganda. It attempts to prevent health problems among young people.

Good or Bad: It Depends on Your Point of View

Are informational programs that are designed to change people's behavior good or bad? Often it depends on your point of view. As first lady, Michelle Obama launched a "Let's Move" program. She wanted kids to eat healthier foods and exercise more. She wanted them to spend less time in front of TV and computer screens. The "Let's Move" message was everywhere. Kids—and parents—saw the information on TV and in schools. Many people applauded Obama's efforts. They believed the program helped fight childhood **obesity**. Others were against the program. They claimed the government was trying to tell families how to live their lives.

Former first lady Michelle Obama enjoyed teaching kids how to exercise.

 obesity—to be extremely overweight

Propaganda is designed to influence how people think. The person or group using it works to make its own point of view sound right. Those who have different opinions are made to seem foolish. Sometimes the people using propaganda refuse to even admit that there are other points of view.

People use many tools to spread propaganda. They choose the tools based on the effect they hope to achieve. Often they play on people's fears. For instance, people fear terrorists striking their hometown. Portraying Muslims as terrorists may cause people to fear or hate *all* Muslims, even though very few have any ties to terrorism.

A Muslim woman tries to combat propaganda with a homemade sign.

COMMON METHODS THAT CAN BE USED IN PROPAGANDA

cherry picking This involves presenting only those facts that support a position and ignoring other facts. This is common in the discussion of controversial issues. Each side presents only the facts on its side of the argument.

loaded words This involves using words that will stir positive or negative reactions in the person who receives the message. Such words could include *patriot* (positive), *terrorist* (negative), or *equality* (positive).

transfer This involves projecting positive or negative qualities on a product or person. For example, showing a candidate standing next to an American flag makes him or her appear to be patriotic.

faulty logic In this approach, a person makes a statement that seems logical until it's looked at more closely. For instance, a person might claim that a blizzard proves there is no global warming. The conclusion is based on a misunderstanding of the difference between climate and weather, or faulty logic.

plain folks This approach appeals to the values of a broad range of people who would consider themselves average. For instance, political campaigns may portray their candidate as being just like the average voter. They might also portray the opponent as being out of touch.

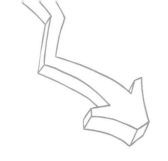

CHAPTER 2

THE HISTORY OF PROPAGANDA

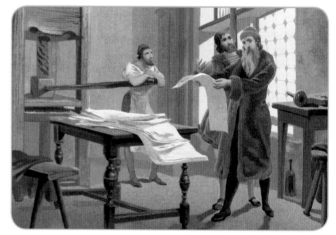

The printing press changed the world.

How long has propaganda been around? All societies have used it to some degree. Ancient Greeks used public plays and speeches to promote their way of life. Ancient Romans used art, writing, and public speeches to praise the power of their empire.

For centuries propaganda spread by word of mouth. Change came with the invention of the Gutenberg printing press around 1440. People could then print many copies of books or flyers stating their views. But the word *propaganda* did not come into use until 200 years later. In 1622 Pope Gregory XV created a group to carry the Catholic faith to new areas. The church set up a College of Propaganda to train priests.

Colonists used propaganda to support their cause.

During the early days of the American Revolution, some colonists favored peace. Others wanted to break away and form a new nation. In early 1776 Thomas Paine published a pamphlet titled "Common Sense." In it he made fun of British royalty and argued for American independence. Readers throughout the colonies bought it. The propaganda pamphlet helped unite people around the cause of independence.

The term propaganda simply meant spreading the faith. Over time the word's meaning changed. It became linked with spreading false information to hurt someone or further a cause.

During the American Revolution, both sides used propaganda. The British tried to convince colonists to remain part of England. Their messages focused on safety and loyalty. Colonists tried to convince people they would be better off without British rule. Their messages focused on freedom and independence.

Throughout history governments have used propaganda during times of war. They prepare messages to boost patriotism among their citizens. They try to create fear among their enemies.

During World War I (1914-1918) the U.S. government came up with a new recruiting poster. It featured Uncle Sam pointing a finger at the viewer. He was saying "I Want YOU for [the] U.S. Army." Uncle Sam was a symbol of the United States. The poster appealed to people's sense of pride in their nation.

I WANT YOU FOR U.S. ARMY
NEAREST RECRUITING STATION

Uncle Sam became the symbol of the U.S. military.

DID YOU KNOW?

Noted movie director Frank Capra and beloved children's book author Dr. Seuss produced propaganda during World War II. Capra directed a series of films called *Why We Fight*. The films were produced to boost public support of the war. Dr. Seuss did a series of political cartoons relating to the war. Some of the cartoons urged people to buy U.S. government bonds to support the war effort.

Frank Capra

During World War II, both sides used propaganda. The United States and its allies focused on the theme of protecting freedom. President Franklin D. Roosevelt rallied public support through speeches. Japan launched a sneak attack on the U.S. naval base in Pearl Harbor, Hawaii, on December 7, 1941. Roosevelt called it "a date which will live in infamy." The words in his speech after the attack prepared the nation for war.

A 1940s U.S. propaganda poster focused on freedom.

 recruit—to enlist someone in the armed forces

 allies—people, groups, or countries that work together for a common cause

 infamy—the state of being well known for a bad quality or action

Japanese Americans were imprisoned by the U.S. government during World War II through no fault of their own.

Both sides played on people's fears during World War II. The U.S. government portrayed the Japanese and German forces they battled against as evil. The propaganda helped maintain public support for the war.

After the Pearl Harbor attack, the U.S. government used fear of Japanese people to place more than 100,000 Japanese Americans in internment camps. They had done nothing wrong. They were imprisoned simply because of their race.

After World War II the Soviet Union gained control of many countries in Eastern Europe. But Soviet leaders wanted more. The Soviet-Russian government wanted to spread its communist form of government across the world. The United States supported governments that believed in capitalism.

The period was called the Cold War. Rather than bombing each other, the countries battled with words. The U.S. used its Voice of America radio network to broadcast information about democracy to listeners in Soviet-controlled countries. The Soviet Union, meanwhile, spread its views that communism was best. Both sides used propaganda.

The Soviet Union broke apart in the early 1990s, but the war of words between Russia and the U.S continues.

 What's in a Name?

Nations even name wars in ways that will boost public support. The war in Iraq in 1991 was named Operation Desert Storm. The term *Desert Storm* suggested that U.S. forces would sweep through Iraq like a storm with little resistance. That proved true.

 internment—to be confined as a prisoner

 communist—a society in which the government, rather than individuals or companies, owns land, factories, and machinery

 capitalism—an economic and political system in which private owners, rather than the government, control business and industry

Propaganda is also an important tool for terrorists. Terror thrives on fear. Groups such as al-Qaida and ISIS send out literature and air broadcasts that demonize the United States. They create videos that promote jihad. Sometimes they show graphic images of their enemies being killed. Their propaganda serves several purposes. The videos are created to scare people around the world, particularly in non-Muslim countries. The propaganda also excites young fighters who might be convinced to join their cause. And it makes those who oppose them afraid to speak out.

The United States and its allies battle terrorists with air strikes and raids targeting their leaders. But they also fight terrorism with words. In late 2016 the Iraqi army began a campaign to recapture the key city of Mosul from ISIS fighters. A U.S.–led coalition provided support. Before the battle, the Iraqi army dropped leaflets over the city. The leaflets promised that the air strikes and the army would "not target civilians." The leaflets urged people to "stay at home" and not listen to rumors spread by ISIS. The leaflets helped combat the propaganda spread by ISIS.

An Iraqi soldier holds a piece of ISIS propaganda that had fallen on the ground.

Because terrorism causes fear, responses to terrorism stress words that focus on safety. After the September 11 attacks in 2001, the United States created a Department of Homeland Security. The word "security" was chosen on purpose. It conveys a sense of people being secure and safe.

⭐ **demonize**—make something or someone seem evil or devilish

⭐ **jihad**—holy war against those who oppose the teachings of Islam

⭐ **coalition**—alliance of people, groups, or countries working together toward a common goal

CHAPTER 3

PROPAGANDA: SHAPING OPINIONS AND ACTIONS

One of the best—or worst—examples of propaganda at work might be politics. Candidates and the groups that support them use many propaganda tools. They try to make themselves look good and their rivals look bad.

For instance, candidates often use loaded language. They portray themselves as patriotic. They say they are hardworking or trustworthy. Meanwhile, candidates try to link their rivals with unpopular words and issues. A candidate might accuse a rival of being a "tax and spend" candidate. But, in doing so, he might leave out information about important services that the taxes funded. Often candidates take brief quotes from a rival out of context. Then they twist the words in ways that make the rival look bad.

Donald Trump's campaign came up with a winning slogan in the 2016 presidential election.

Candidates also try to come up with catchy campaign slogans. In 2016 presidential candidate Donald Trump used the slogan "Make America Great Again." It worked in several ways. It captured the sense that all citizens want America to be great. The word *again* suggested that change was needed to return the country to greatness. The slogan also suggested that Trump was the person who could bring the change.

Politicians use ad campaigns to get elected. Public service ad campaigns promote worthy causes. Companies use ad campaigns to sell products or services. In all cases, the communicators present information about themselves in the best possible light. Sometimes that information is twisted in ways that are untrue or unfair. Then it becomes propaganda.

Examples of ad campaigns that spread "good propaganda" are those of the Advertising Council. The council's ads have promoted a variety of worthy causes. Through its ads, Smokey the Bear urged people to help prevent wildfires. McGruff the Crime Dog taught people about crime prevention. Crash test dummies urged proper seat belt usage. The ads use strong feelings and dramatic images to shape opinion and encourage positive actions.

Smokey the Bear has become a well-known symbol of fire prevention.

FAMOUS POLITICAL SLOGANS AND ADS HELPED PRESIDENTIAL CANDIDATES WIN

Slogans

"DON'T SWAP HORSES WHEN CROSSING STREAMS"
Abraham Lincoln (for re-election, 1864)

"HAPPY DAYS ARE HERE AGAIN"
Franklin D. Roosevelt, 1932

"I LIKE IKE"
Dwight D. Eisenhower, 1952

"ALL THE WAY WITH LBJ"
Lyndon Baines Johnson, 1964

"CHANGE WE CAN BELIEVE IN"
Barack Obama, 2008

Ads

"Morning in America"
Ronald Reagan, 1984. The positive re-election ad began, "It's morning in America again." Then it listed ways life in the U.S. had become better during the four years Reagan had been president.

"Yes, We Can"
Barack Obama, 2008. The four-minute ad combined Obama's words with the singing of pop stars and celebrities. It received an Emmy Award for best web video on daytime TV.

CHAPTER 4

PROPAGANDA TODAY

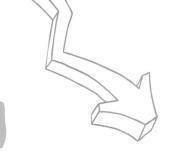

The Internet makes many things easier. Shopping is easier. Connecting with people is easier. Finding information on any topic is easier. But is the information you find correct? Anyone can create a website or blog. That makes it easier than ever for people to post propaganda.

We've all heard about messages going viral. It happens when people share a video, tweet, or idea that captures their interest. If enough people share the message, the wave of popularity may cause it to go viral. When we hear the phrase "going viral" we often think of videos of cute babies and animals. But businesses also create video clips, text messages, and tweets they hope will go viral. Political parties use similar methods to promote candidates.

The Internet has also blurred the line between real news and fake news. Fake news is false information or propaganda disguised as a real news story. Often the stories have sensational headlines designed to get people to read more. As with propaganda, the way people use this term has changed. The term means false news purposely designed to deceive people. But many politicians and others now use the term to dismiss any news they don't agree with. Denying the value of real news is a form of propaganda itself.

The spreading of false information makes it hard to know what is real.

 Chinese Propaganda Goes Viral

For many years China has been known for blocking Internet sites such as Facebook and Google. Now the Chinese government is using social media to spread propaganda. The government has produced animated videos of President Xi Jinping. It has created music videos for kids. It's even working with a Chinese hip-hop group to release songs that praise China and criticize the United States.

In 2015 and 2016 Russian agents worked to influence the 2016 U.S. presidential election. They hacked into Democratic National Committee computers. They released thousands of emails designed to make Democratic presidential candidate Hillary Clinton look bad.

Meanwhile, paid Russian social media **trolls** posted millions of messages on Facebook and Twitter. Many of the posts were designed to divide U.S. voters. Russian posts and videos reached more than 100 million people. Although we may never fully know how much the ads influenced the 2016 presidential election, we know that they did.

How can you tell if something is news at all, or simply propaganda? Start by asking several questions. First, what is the purpose of the information? Is someone trying to influence your thoughts and actions? Does the source benefit in some way? Does the message ask you to buy a product or support a certain cause? If so, the information may be propaganda.

Next, ask yourself who is posting the message. Sometimes it can be hard to tell. Propagandists often hide their true identity. Careful reading can help. Many spelling mistakes or a poor grasp of English

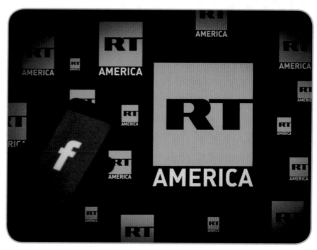

Russian media used Facebook to influence the 2016 presidential election in the U.S.

grammar may be a sign that the source of the information is not trustworthy.

Then, check to see if the message uses any common propaganda methods. Does it present data in an unfair way? Does it use loaded words? Does it make fun of opposing points of view without providing facts? If it does one or more of these things, it probably qualifies as propaganda.

 troll—a person who tries to start arguments on the Internet by posting false information or angry statements

You may see propaganda used at school. Maybe your classmates are promoting their points of view on an issue. They present only those facts that support their cause. Or maybe someone has spread false information about a classmate. That propaganda may damage someone's reputation.

In the Internet age, people must process more information and propaganda than ever before. There is little tolerance for opposing viewpoints. Twitter and Facebook debates rage on issues such as immigration, guns, health care, and racism. In each case, people who post on social media sites focus on information that supports their own opinions.

Some NFL players knelt during the national anthem to protest injustice against people of color. Football fans were divided in their reactions.

How do you separate facts from propaganda? First, never assume something is true just because you see it in print or online. Check other sources for agreement. News coverage differs greatly among sources.

Read critically. Learn to figure out who is presenting the information and why. As you read, make sure that facts are presented fairly and correctly. Watch for propaganda methods. See if word choice is being used to shape your opinion. Check whether the information shows bias against a person, group, or belief. Remain open to hearing information and opinions you disagree with.

By being a critical consumer of information, you can protect yourself from being deceived. Being able to recognize propaganda allows you to study the information and take proper action.

 tolerance—seeing that your way isn't the only way

 bias—favoring one person or point of view over another

GLOSSARY

allies (a-LYZ)—people, groups, or countries that work together for a common cause

bias (BYE-uhs)—favoring one person or point of view over another

capitalism (KA-puh-tuhl-iz-im)—an economic and political system in which private owners, rather than the government, control business and industry

coalition (koh-uh-LISH-uhn)—alliance of people, groups, or countries working together toward a common goal

communist (KAHM-yuh-nizt)—a society in which the government, rather than individuals or companies, owns land, factories, and machinery

demonize (DE-men-ize)—make something or someone seem evil or devilish

infamy (IN-fah-me)—the state of being well known for a bad quality or action

internment (IN-turn-meant)—to be confined as a prisoner

jihad (jee-HAD)—a holy war against those who oppose the teachings of Islam

obesity (oh-BEE-si-tee)—to be extremely overweight

propaganda (PROP-uh-gan-duh)—information spread to try to influence the thinking of people; often not completely true or fair

recruit (ri-KROOT)—to enlist someone in the armed forces

tolerance (TOLL-ur-anz)—seeing that your way isn't the only way

troll (TROHL)—a person who tries to start arguments on the Internet by posting false information or angry statements

READ MORE

Dakers, Diane. *Information Literacy and Fake News.* St. Catharines, Ontario: Crabtree, 2018.

Hand, Carol. *Everything You Need to Know about Fake News and Propaganda.* New York: Rosen, 2018.

Shoup, Katie. *Nazi Propaganda: Jews in Hitler's Germany.* New York: Rosen, 2017.

CRITICAL THINKING QUESTIONS

1. How do governments and political candidates running for office use propaganda in similar ways?
2. What are some questions people can ask themselves to determine whether information is propaganda?
3. How has the way people use the term "fake news" changed in recent years, and how does that relate to propaganda?

INTERNET SITES

Use FactHound to find Internet sites related to this book.

1. Visit *www.facthound.com*
2. Just type in 9781543527056 and go.

Super-cool stuff! Check out projects, games and lots more at
www.capstonekids.com

INDEX